THIS BOOK BELONGS TO:

Stevie Colbert

BUT HE HOPES
YOU, _____,
READ AND ENJOY IT.

AFTER ALL, YOU'RE
THE GREATEST
_____ POLE
IN THE WORLD!

I AM A POLE
(AND SO CAN YOU!)

by STEPHEN COLBERT

with illustrations by
PAUL HILDEBRAND

GRAND CENTRAL
PUBLISHING

New York   Boston

I AM A POLE
(AND SO CAN YOU!)

WRITTEN AND EDITED BY
Stephen Colbert and Aaron Cohen

WITH CONTRIBUTIONS FROM
Paul Dinello, Rob Dubbin, and Scott Sherman

ILLUSTRATIONS BY
Paul Hildebrand

SPECIAL THANKS TO
Liz Russomanno-Doyle and Maurice Sendak

BOOK DESIGN BY
Aaron Cohen and Paul Hildebrand
Cover based on design by Doyle Partners

BACK COVER PHOTOGRAPH BY
Andrew Matheson

Copyright © 2012 by Spartina Productions, Inc.
Grand Central Publishing   Hachette Book Group   237 Park Avenue   New York, NY 10017
www.HachetteBookGroup.com
Printed in the United States of America
WOR
First Edition: May 2012
10 9 8 7 6 5 4 3 2 1
Grand Central Publishing is a division of Hachette Book Group, Inc.
The Grand Central Publishing name and logo is a trademark of Hachette Book Group, Inc.
The publisher is not responsible for websites (or their content) that are not owned by the publisher. The Hachette Speakers Bureau provides a wide range of authors for speaking events. To find out more, go to www.hachettespeakersbureau.com or call (866) 376-6591.
ISBN 978-1-455-52342-9

*For poles everywhere–
keep dreaming*

I AM A POLE!

That much is clear to me...
But just what type of pole,
Is it I should be?

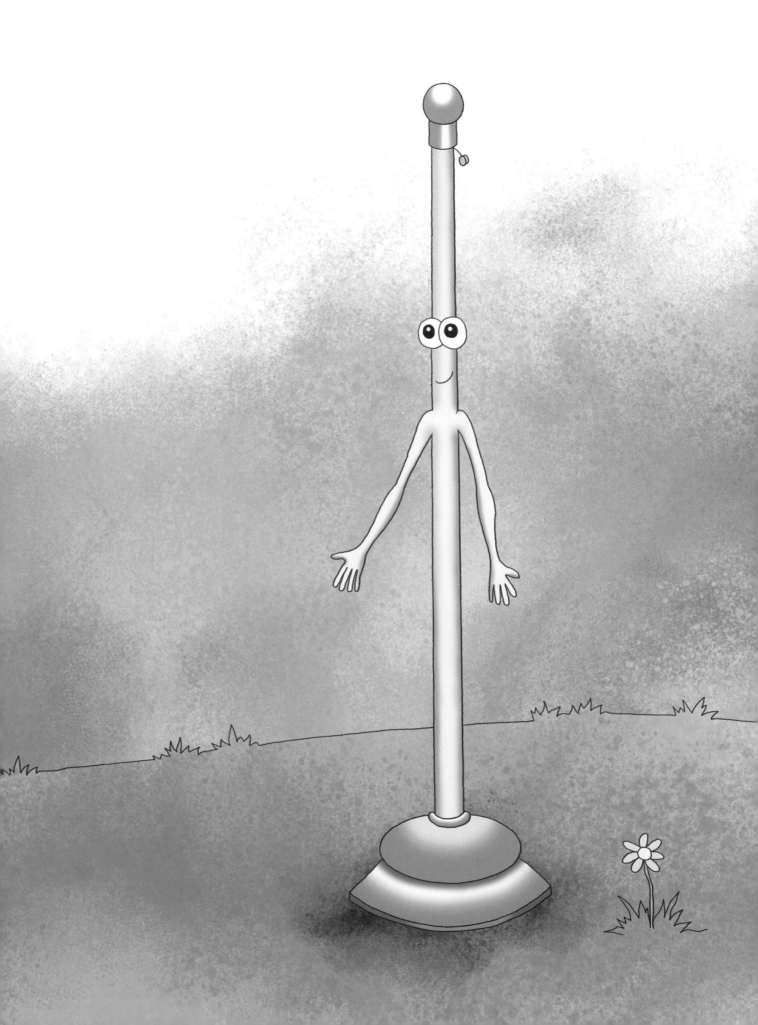

I know I have a purpose,
I'm sure this may sound odd:
But a pole without a job to do,
Is really just a rod.*

So I've spent a lot of time,
In pursuit of one clear goal:
Finding out where I fit in.
What is my true pole role?

*For the record, some of my best friends are rods. Between you and me, they're a lot better than sticks.**
**Don't get me started on sticks.

My cousin Bob's a lamp pole,
But he doesn't seem that bright.
So what is it that I can do?
There must be something... right?

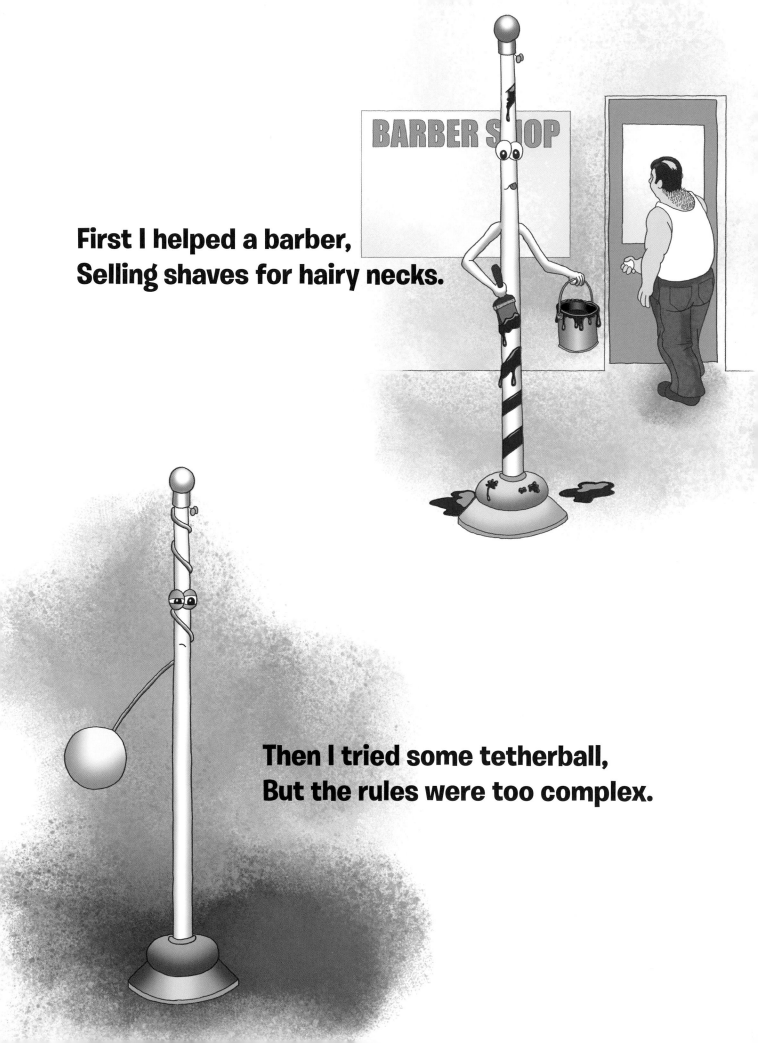

First I helped a barber,
Selling shaves for hairy necks.

Then I tried some tetherball,
But the rules were too complex.

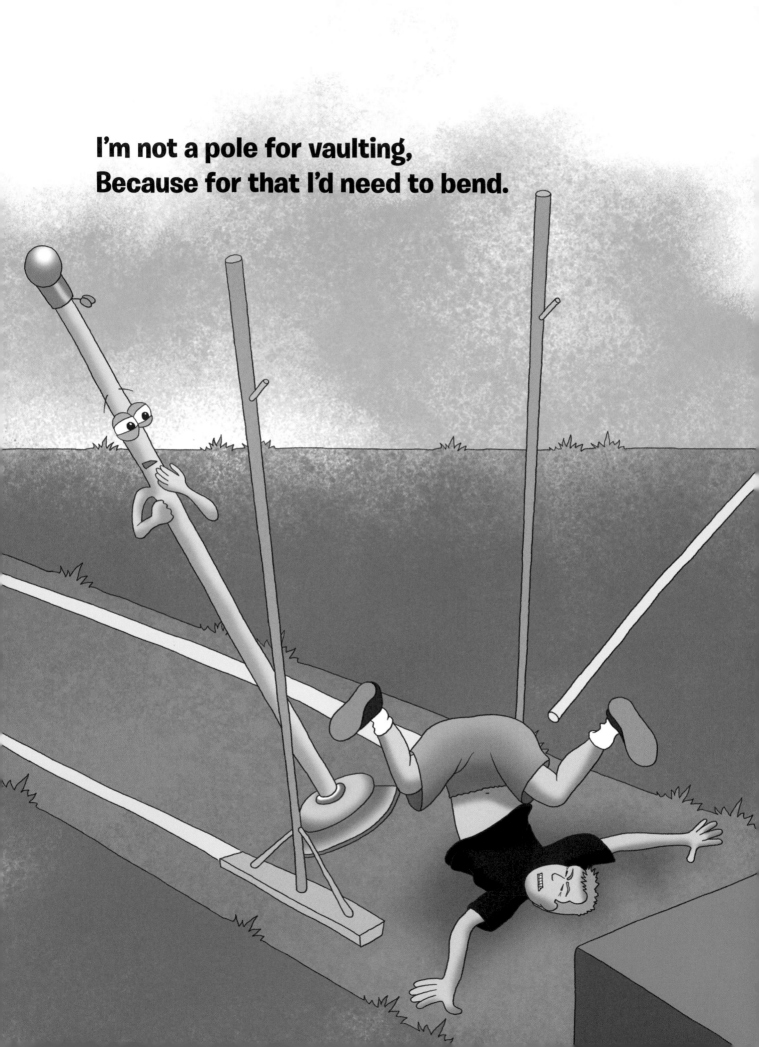

I'm not a pole for vaulting,
Because for that I'd need to bend.

**And I'd love to be a ski pole,
But for that I'd need a friend.**

**Or even just a Gallup® poll,
Calling voters in Atlanta.**

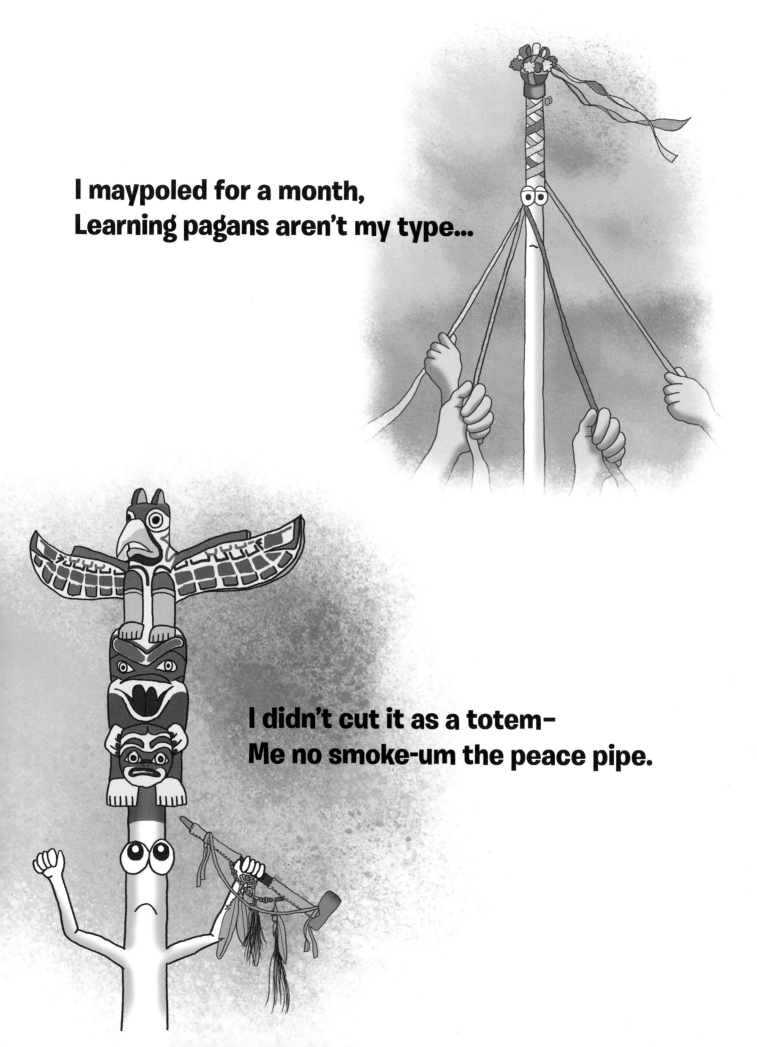

I told myself that tadpole
Was a possible solution.

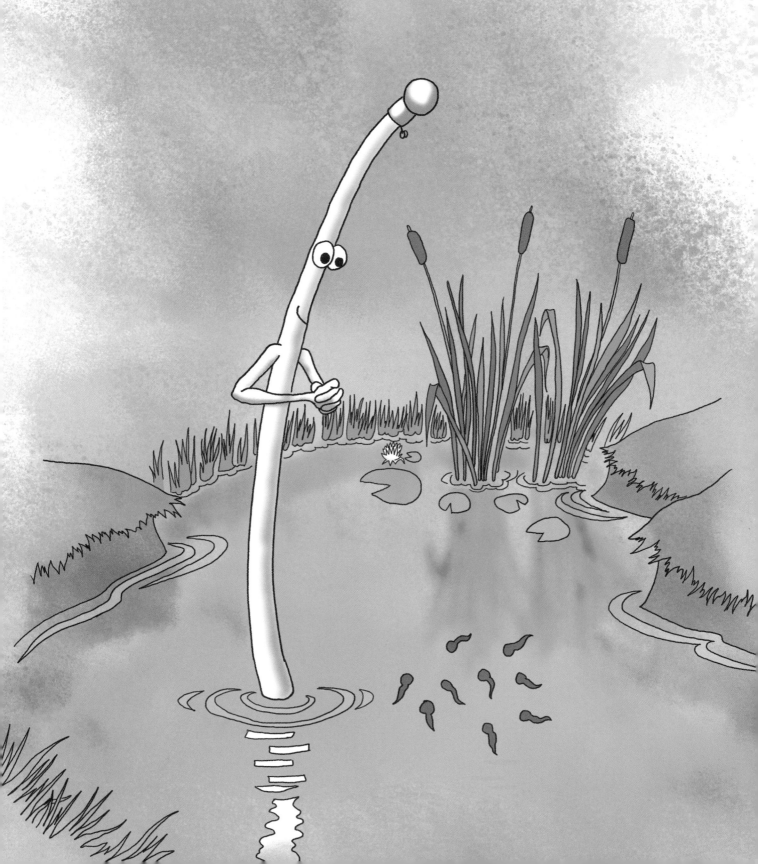

**That didn't work out either–
Goshdarnit, evolution!**

I briefly was a poleax,
For a brave medieval knight-
It turns out I'm not that sharp,
And I'm much too scared to fight.

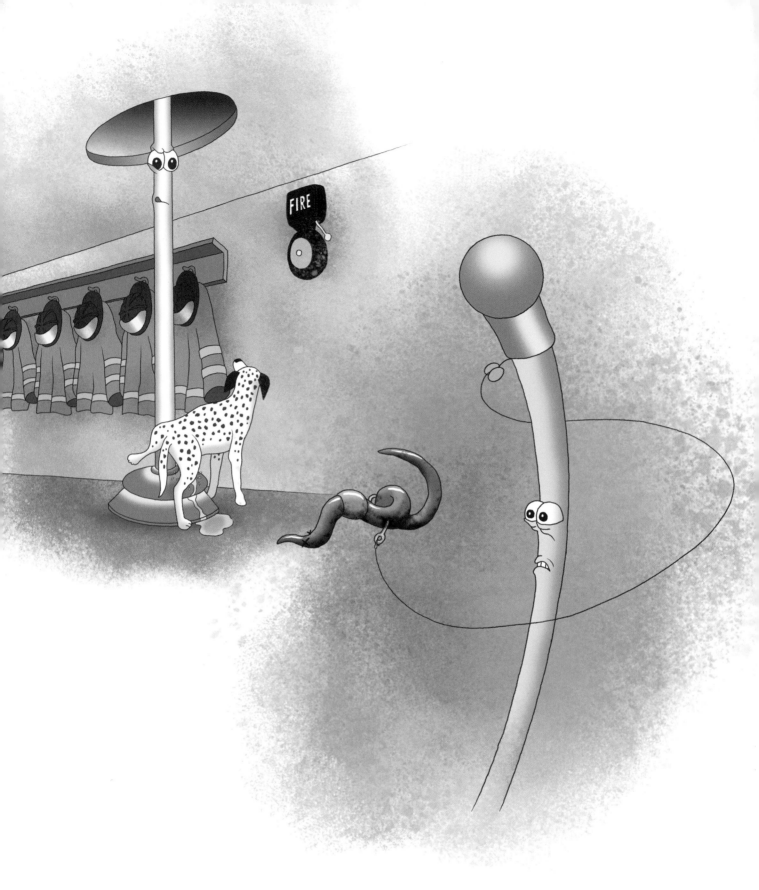

**There's always fireman's or fishing,
But those jobs are hard to find.**

So I interned as a stripper pole,
But I couldn't stand the grind.

**I tried and failed at other things,
That I shouldn't talk about.**

Like that summer with the phone poles,
Getting totally strung out.

For people it seems easy
To find a role that suits you most,
Like a job of true importance,
Such as late night TV host.

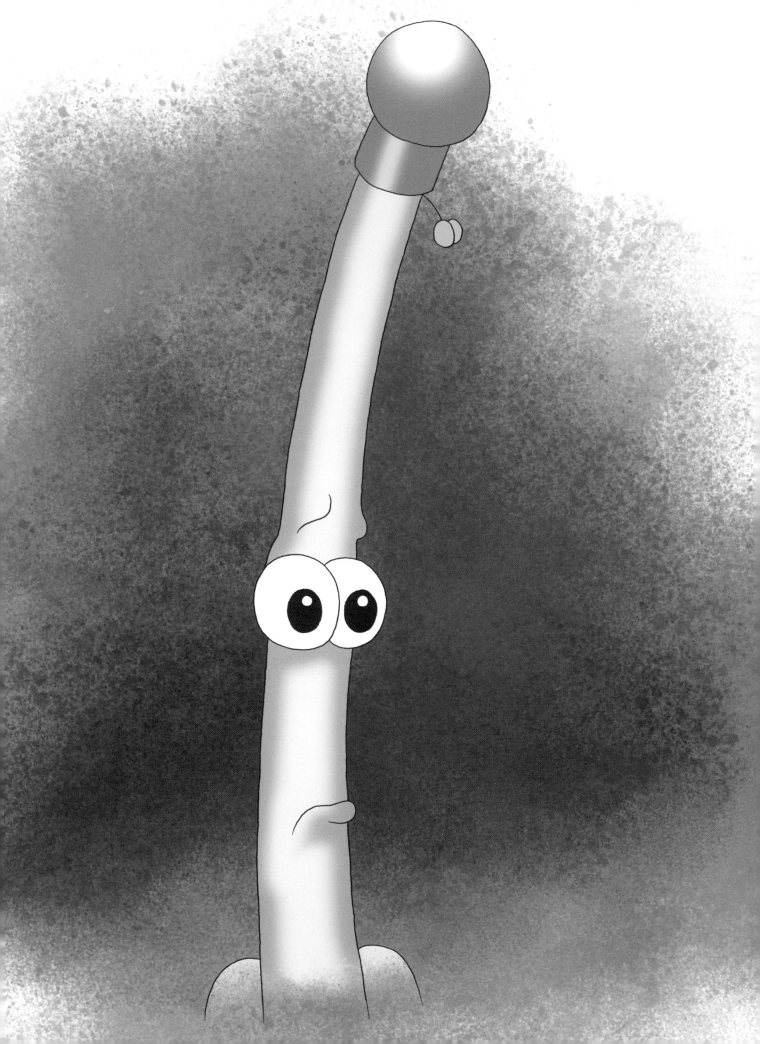

But I don't have that option.
And from what I can deduce,
The only pole I'm going to be,
Is one with no good use.

It seems that there's no place for me.
Forget I ever spoke.
I guess I'm just a punch line,
To some awful pole-ish joke.

BUT, WAIT!

Who is this that I see coming,
In the depths of my despair?
Some scouts bringing "Old Glory,"
As a frock for me to wear!

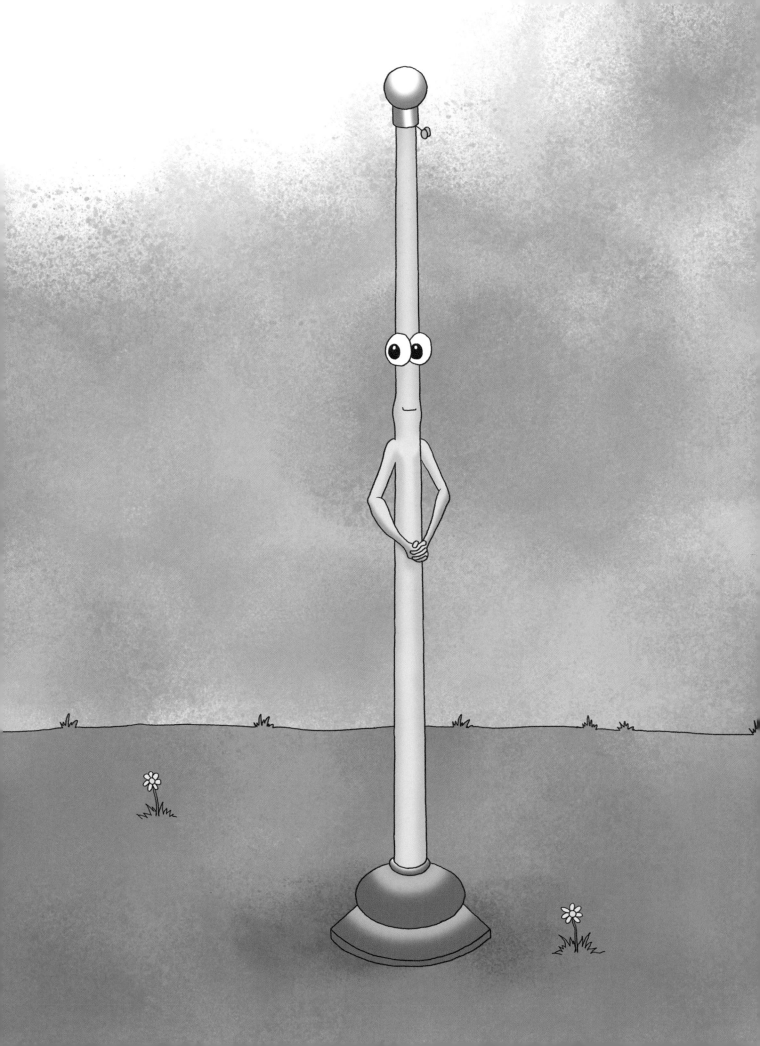

I've always thought red, white, and blue
Went nicely with my eyes.
And horizontal stripes sure do
Show off my shapely thighs.

As she dances and she waves,
It is finally clear to see,
I'm the very best kind of pole
I could ever hope to be...

I AM AN AMERICAN FLAG POLE!

So pledge allegiance... to me!

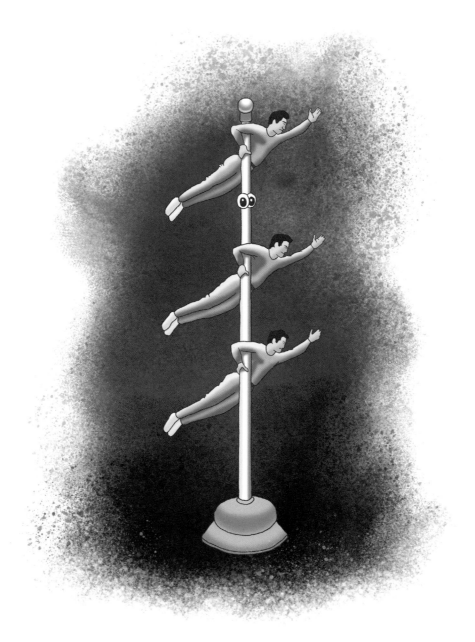

(Based on a true story.)

SHOW US YOUR POLE!

DRAW OR TRACE YOUR POLE HERE

STEPHEN COLBERT, age 47

MAURICE SENDAK, age 83